Liberty Phi

SAGITTARIUS

INTRODUCTION

Astrology is all about the planets in our skies and what energy and characteristics influence us. From ancient times, people have wanted to understand the rhythms of life and looked to the skies and their celestial bodies for inspiration, and the ancient constellations are there in the 12 zodiac signs we recognise from astrology. The Ancient Greeks devised narratives related to myths and legends about their celestial ancestors, to which they referred to make decisions and choices. Roman mythology did the same and over the years these ancient wisdoms became refined into today's modern astrology.

The configuration of the planets in the sky at the time and place of our birth is unique to each and every one of us, and what this means and how it plays out throughout our lives is both fascinating and informative. Just knowing which planet rules your sun sign is the beginning of an exploratory journey that can provide you with a useful tool for life.

Understanding the meaning, energetic nature and power of each planet, where this sits in your birth chart and what this might mean is all important information and linked to your date, place and time of birth, relevant *only* to you. Completely individual, the way in which you can work with the power of the planets comes from understanding their qualities and how this might influence the position in which they sit in your chart.

What knowledge of astrology can give you is the tools for working out how a planetary pattern might influence you, because of its relationship to your particular planetary configuration and circumstances. Each sun sign has a set of characteristics linked to its ruling planet – for example, Sagittarius is ruled by Jupiter – and, in turn, to each of the 12 Houses (see page 81) that form the structure of every individual's birth chart (see page 78). Once you know the meanings of these and how these relate to different areas of your life, you can begin to work out what might be relevant to you when, for example, you read in a magazine horoscope that there's a Full Moon in Capricorn or that Jupiter is transiting Mars.

Each of the 12 astrological or zodiac sun signs is ruled by a planet (see page 52) and looking at a planet's characteristics will give you an indication of the influences brought to bear on each sign. It's useful to have a general understanding of these influences, because your birth chart includes many of them, in different house or planetary configurations, which gives you information about how uniquely *you* you are. Also included in this book are the minor planets (see page 102), also relevant to the information your chart provides.

SAGITTARIUS

Our sun sign is determined by the date of our birth wherever we are born, and if you are a Sagittarius you were born between November 22nd and December 21st. Bear in mind, however, that if you were born on one or other of those actual dates it's worth checking your *time* of birth, if you know it, against the year you were born and where. That's because no one is born 'on the cusp' (see page 78) and because there will be a moment on those days when Scorpio shifts to Sagittarius, and Sagittarius shifts to Capricorn. It's well worth a check, especially if you've never felt quite convinced that the characteristics of your designated sun sign match your own.

The constellation of Sagittarius, the Latin word for archer, is one of the largest in our skies and its brightest star is Epsilon Sagittarii, meaning the bottom of the (archer's) bow. Said to represent the Greek god Crotus, the original Sagittarius was a great hunter and excelled at archery. And when Sagittarius was placed in the sky, he was given additional legs to show he was also a great horseman.

Sagittarius is ruled by the planet Jupiter, the largest planet in the solar system. It takes 12 years to transit the Sun, spending around a year in each sun sign, enhancing and expanding on each sign's qualities with its optimism and abundance.

A fire sign (like Aries and Leo), Sagittarius has great positive energy, and approaches life with enthusiasm and optimism. It takes quite a lot to knock their self-confidence, as Jupiter is all about trusting in the future, generosity and tolerance. Sagittarius is also a mutable sign (like Gemini, Virgo and Pisces) and is consequently very good at adapting to circumstances and situations, making the best of every opportunity and possibility. This tendency to always be hopeful and positive can sometimes veer over into blind optimism that can occasionally shake Sagittarius' confidence, which can also make them come across as irresponsible from time to time. Irresponsibility with their own time, money or possessions is one thing, but if this extends to that of others, it can cause exasperation and irritation in their relationships.

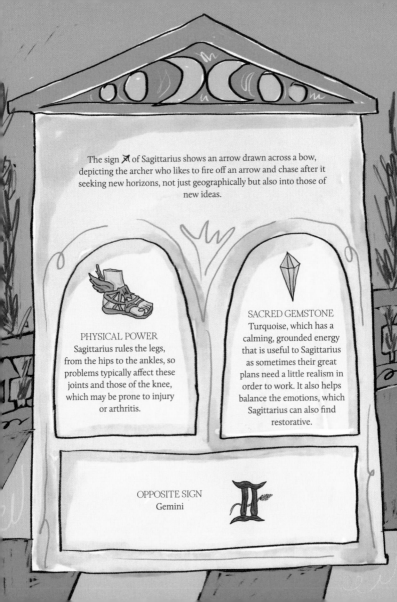

The sign ⚹ of Sagittarius shows an arrow drawn across a bow, depicting the archer who likes to fire off an arrow and chase after it seeking new horizons, not just geographically but also into those of new ideas.

PHYSICAL POWER
Sagittarius rules the legs, from the hips to the ankles, so problems typically affect these joints and those of the knee, which may be prone to injury or arthritis.

SACRED GEMSTONE
Turquoise, which has a calming, grounded energy that is useful to Sagittarius as sometimes their great plans need a little realism in order to work. It also helps balance the emotions, which Sagittarius can also find restorative.

OPPOSITE SIGN
Gemini

Sagittarius is depicted by the archer, shooting arrows into the distance and chasing after them, and also by the centaur, half-man and half-horse. Sagittarius is the sign of the traveller both in body and mind, constantly seeking new geographical, physical or intellectual horizons to explore.

Sagittarius can sometimes appear to breeze through life, fuelled by optimism and enthusiasm, the gift of their ruling planet Jupiter. Somehow, doors always seem to open in front of Sagittarius' cheerful approach, giving the impression that they always travel under a lucky star. Part of this impression is because when things do go wrong, Sagittarius just moves on and is much more interested in seeing what it is possible to achieve, rather than analysing what isn't. Not wasting time on things that can't be changed, and focusing on what can, is very much Sagittarius' philosophy, and it frees up a lot of time for them if they are not sitting around fretting or ruminating on what didn't work.

The downside of this is that Sagittarius can sometimes come across as irresponsible or frivolous, leaving a trail of unfinished business or broken promises in their wake. This is not their intention, but many Sagittarius hold the view that 'least said, soonest mended' applies and there is no point in crying over spilt milk, so they just get on with it and move on. It can be a very useful, if brisk, approach and many find that Sagittarius is straightforward to a fault in this way, without resorting to guile or subterfuge. And Sagittarius also has no problem with others taking the same line; acting passive-aggressively isn't really how this sign operates.

Independence and curiosity are key traits too. This combination often finds Sagittarius keen to go it alone to explore their interests. They love company, but unless that company can keep up, Sagittarius will take off by themselves, happy to make new friends or acquire fellow travellers along the way. This applies as much to physical travel as to the exploration of new ideas, and many Sagittarius are constant students or opt to pursue studies outside their immediate area of expertise, building on these, contributing to them and taking it all as far as it will go. In turn, this keeps Sagittarius youthful in their attitude, happy to sample new music, art and ideas.

This highly adaptable, optimistic and occasionally ebullient sign of Sagittarius is also something of a philosopher, and they love to share their ideas and thoughts with others. For them, a stranger is just a friend they've not yet met and their open-heartedness is one of their most likeable traits. As family, friend or lover, Sagittarius is rarely bored or boring and this makes them very attractive to be around, so they are seldom short of company and often to be found socialising.

THE MOON IN YOUR CHART

While your zodiac sign is your sun sign, making you a sun sign Sagittarius, the Moon also plays a role in your birth chart and if you know the time and place of your birth, along with your birth date, you can get your birth chart done (see page 78). From this you can discover in which zodiac sign your Moon is positioned in your chart.

The Moon reflects the characteristics of who you are at the time of your birth, your innate personality, how you express yourself and how you are seen by others. This is in contrast to our sun sign which indicates the more dominant characteristics we reveal as we travel through life. The Moon also represents the feminine in our natal chart (the Sun the masculine) and the sign in which our Moon falls can indicate how we express the feminine side of our personality. Looking at the two signs together in our charts immediately creates a balance.

MOON IN SAGITTARIUS

The Moon spends roughly 2.5 days in each zodiac sign as it moves through all 12 signs during its monthly cycle. This means that the Moon is regularly in Sagittarius, and it can be useful to know when this occurs and in particular when we have a New Moon or a Full Moon in Sagittarius because these are especially good times for you to focus your energy and intentions.

A New Moon is always the start of a new cycle, an opportunity to set new intentions for the coming month, and when this is in your own sign, Sagittarius, you can benefit from this additional energy and support. The Full Moon is an opportunity to reflect on the culmination of your earlier intentions.

NEW MOON
IN SAGITTARIUS AFFIRMATION

'Every journey begins with a first step and I will
trust in the Moon's inspiration today and tomorrow,
moving forward until I realise my goal.'

FULL MOON
IN SAGITTARIUS AFFIRMATION

'I trust in the culmination of what might be the first
stage in exploration and if things are not yet clear to
me, I will look to the horizon and the bigger picture.'

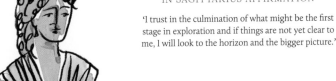

SAGITTARIUS HEALTH

Sagittarius rules the lower limbs, from hip joint to that of the little toe, making legs, ankles and feet susceptible to injury or illness. Physical activity is a priority for many Sagittarius, so they need to ensure they take care of their joints, as knees in particular can be vulnerable. All that rushing around can also make accidents possible, with sprains, strains or fractures a possibility.

An enjoyment of physical activity is a feature of many Sagittarius' lives, although formal exercise might be too much of a restraint for some. Running independently wild in one way or another is much more Sagittarius' style, although some actively enjoy the sociability of team sports as long as they can occupy pole position. What many Sagittarius do need, however, is a balance between physical activity and mental calm, otherwise there can be a tendency to burn out. For a fire sign, swimming isn't an obvious choice but it does support the joints while exercising the limbs and building stamina. What Sagittarius might enjoy then is wild swimming, where rules and restrictive swimming lanes don't apply. And when it comes to any necessary recovery, strength and stamina can be regained through gentler forms of exercise.

POWER UP YOUR SAGITTARIUS ENERGY

There are often moments or periods when we feel uninspired, demotivated and low in energy. At these times it's worth working with your innate sun sign energy to power up again, and paying attention to what Sagittarius relishes and needs can help support both physical and mental health.

Sagittarius' fiery energy and rushing from pillar to post on new projects is all very stimulating and exhilarating, but there will come a time when it's necessary for them to rest and recuperate. This may even be because of an injury, when it's important to allow adequate time for broken bones or ligament sprains to heal, but it can be equally necessary to avoid becoming psychologically overwhelmed and played out. No one, not even Sagittarius, can burn the candle at both ends forever.

As an adaptable fire sign ruled by optimistic Jupiter, it's sometimes helpful to seek out calming and soothing ways to recharge the batteries. Gentle walks through nature, yoga and meditation, listening to music or reading, and occupations like bird watching or watercolour painting that require stillness and observation, will all help Sagittarius reset their internal stress thermostat, whether they think they need to or not. And many won't recognise the need until they crash. Ignoring early warning signs is a mistake; one of the first principles of self-care is to know your own body and mind and be mindful of them. Being unable to sleep isn't usually a problem for Sagittarius, but if insomnia or early morning waking occurs, it can be a sign that all's not well. Aching legs and joints can also disrupt sleep. It's always good for Sagittarius to keep some arnica handy too, both as an oral homeopathic remedy and also as a cream.

Reassessing their work/life balance can be a first step in self-care for Sagittarius. And that balance also needs to include regular hours and regular meals, both of which Sagittarius can easily forget. This includes a balanced diet too, with low-glycaemic carbs, enough protein and lots of fresh fruit and vegetables. Magnesium might be a missing element, causing muscular cramps in the legs, and good sources for that include brown rice, chicken breast, avocadoes, broccoli, spinach, bananas, almonds and oats – basically all the dietary goodies. Herbs and spices that resonate with Sagittarius energy to refresh the palate include chervil, arnica, nutmeg, saffron and star anise, which all help restore vigour.

Utilise a New Moon in Sagittarius with a ritual to set your intentions and power up: light a candle, use essential oil of chamomile to help calm fiery energy (this oil blends well with soothing lavender and uplifting vetiver), focus your thoughts on the change you wish to see and allow time to meditate on this. Place your gemstone (see page 13) in the moonlight. Write down your intentions and keep in a safe place. Meditate on the New Moon in Sagittarius affirmation (see page 21).

At a Full Moon in Sagittarius you will have the benefit of the sun's reflected light to help illuminate what is working for you and what you can let go, because the Full Moon brings clarity. Take the time to meditate on the Full Moon in Sagittarius affirmation (see page 21). Light a candle, place your gemstone in the moonlight and make a note of your thoughts and feelings, strengthened by the Moon in your sign.

SAGITTARIUS'
SPIRITUAL
HOME

Knowing where to go to replenish your soul and recharge your batteries both physically and spiritually is important and worth serious consideration. For some Sagittarius, their spiritual home will always be somewhere they can travel to and explore, either in reality or in their heads. For others, it will be a home they've created that showcases their past travels.

Wherever they hail from or end up, there are also a number of countries where Sagittarius will feel comfortable, whether they choose to go there to live, work or just take a holiday. For the open-minded Sagittarius, the wide-open spaces of Canada, South Africa and Costa Rica allow for an invigorating mix of nature and cultural attractions, irrespective of where Sagittarius was born. Shorter-term visits or holidays usually include an element of exploration, and whether it's Stuttgart, Naples or Acapulco, there must be an opportunity for Sagittarius to meet with local people and enjoy the culture.

S A G I T

W O M A N

W O

T A R I U S

When Sagittarius women come into the room, heads turn. There's an immediate vivacity that attracts the eye, and she is seldom short of admirers as she trots through life. It's often her buoyant enthusiasm and outgoing nature that is so immediately obvious, and even the shyest of Sagittarius (there are some) seem to find it easy to engage with others. Consequently, it's almost impossible to resist being drawn into her ideas or plans, even when they are a little unrealistic. But it's where she starts from and the details can be worked out later, often by someone else, or even abandoned as a new thought beckons. Restless by nature, when things don't work out immediately, there's usually another project or person to focus on.

Many find her hard to keep up with and some fall by the wayside, but few people are anything other than impressed by Sagittarius woman's enthusiasm for whatever she sets her mind to or her heart upon. Her approach is as straightforward as the arrow from the bow, and this in itself is disarming. If she likes you, you'll know, whether you're a work colleague, friend or potential lover. For some that can be quite alarming and, as she matures, a

Sagittarius woman may need to learn to temper her approach with a little gentleness and humility to win people over fully.

Her style is often as individual as her take on life, but Sagittarius women tend towards clothes that express their need to move swiftly, so those vertiginous designer heels are seldom for everyday wear. There may be something rather brisk and functional about those tailored jackets, but there's often a flame-coloured accessory to signal that Sagittarius energy. Good-quality garments that last are often a priority, and she is happy to mix vintage with high street to achieve her own personalised Sagittarius look, so her basic wardrobe is often sleekly assembled.

A friendly streak makes a Sagittarius woman instantly approachable, and she's a good friend who will want to invite you along on her adventures and won't mind if you're not available or interested. She can adapt to many situations and is happiest when life is busy. Her spontaneity and curiosity open many doors, ensuring that exploration and adventures are always possible for her.

SAGIT

MAN

TARIUS

He tends to come across as somewhat larger than life, does Sagittarius man, jovial and open-hearted, happy to volunteer to help in any circumstance, curious about you and your life. Everyone needs a friend like this. Make the most of him when he's around, however, because chances are he's not around for long. It may be work or it may be for fun, but this is a man who is often in pursuit of adventure, as his Sagittarius spirit thrives on this.

This is also a man who seems to move in a straight line, seldom deviating from what his Sagittarius mind is currently focused on, at least for as long as it serves its purpose of keeping him interested. There is no shortage of fiery energy when his curiosity is piqued, but the other side of this is a low boredom threshold, something Sagittarius men have to learn to manage as they mature. Otherwise, how will they ever complete anything?

Adaptation is also the name of this man's game, and Sagittarius is a mutable sign, so they are able to utilise their optimism and enthusiasm to get others onside, often taking a lot of trouble to support others through difficult times. This is a lovely Sagittarius trait, often overlooked, but these men can be very positive role models and great cheerleaders with greater sticking power than they are often given credit for. Restless spirits yes, but their heart is strong and true and for those they love they can be stalwart in their support.

His range of interests is often huge, so finding a point of contact to initiate a conversation is usually easy with Sagittarius men, plus they are by nature genuinely and straightforwardly friendly. There's not much side to Sagittarius, what you see is what you get, and they seldom play emotional games which can be refreshing. However, keeping up with them is less easy, as they are constantly drawn to a journey whether in body or mind.

SAGITTARIUS IN LOVE

L ove is important to Sagittarius and burns brightly for them,
    but it is often not the be-all and end-all of their existence
    as it is for some. They love being in love, but this can
happen regularly, as they fall in love easily and often without much
thought of its future – because, in reality for Sagittarius, love is
seldom future-proofed. The future is often another country, not
yet explored and who knows what they will find there? Often with
Sagittarius, what starts out as a mutual friendship based on shared
interests, turns into love. There is seldom a prototype for Sagittarius,
and their choice of lover can be diverse. But as long as those shared
interests develop and grow, keeping Sagittarius interested, chances
are that love will endure and the journey can be continued together.

SAGITTARIUS AS A LOVER

Sagittarius is as curious about sex as anything else, but with an open-minded and exploratory approach that's usually very straightforward. Eroticism is important too, but Sagittarius also likes authenticity and spontaneity.

Some Sagittarius aren't averse to having several partners at the same time because, as they might say, variety is the spice of life and it reduces the risk of boredom. Certainly, few Sagittarius have many reservations about playing the field before settling down, and often a friendship can segue into a love match, because friendship lies at the core of what makes an intimate relationship work for Sagittarius. This is because Sagittarius has a tendency to be very independently minded, so anything that smacks of possessiveness or restriction can be a real turn-off and, because of this, needy lovers shouldn't apply. Too much pressure and that centaur is likely to bolt. Shared interests outside the bedroom help reduce the pressure on Sagittarius that many will find reassuring, and this can provide an enduring anchor for the romance.

Sex for Sagittarius isn't just physical though; they also need to be mentally stimulated by their partner otherwise the relationship is unlikely to last. This component of sexual attration isn't always obvious to Sagittarius themselves, but without it the relationship is unlikely to last. This means that lovers are often met through work or study, shared pastimes or activities, seldom through random online dating. That's not to say that online dating isn't possible for Sagittarius, but it's only in the meeting of minds that real attraction occurs, because it seldom comes down to the superficial with this sign. Authenticity matters and few Sagittarius will pursue a relationship without it.

WHAT'S IN SAGITTARIUS' BEDSIDE CABINET?

A vintage riding crop

Silken ties

Sandalwood-infused massage oil

WHICH SIGN SUITS SAGITTARIUS?

In relationships with Sagittarius, the sun sign of the other person and the ruling planet of that sign can bring out the best, or sometimes the worst, in a lover. Knowing what might spark, smoulder or suffocate love is worth closer investigation, but always remember that sun sign astrology is only a starting point for any relationship.

SAGITTARIUS
AND ARIES

Fire and fire, Mars and Jupiter, there's
a huge combustible energy here that
both signs recognise and relish and
bond over, but it usually needs to be
tempered with a little gentleness to
work, otherwise the relationship could,
quite literally, burn out.

SAGITTARIUS
AND TAURUS

Lovely, grounded Venus is more
than a match for Jupiter, the planet
of expansion and enthusiasm, and
this combination can be truly life-
enhancing for both as long as they pay
attention to the need for a degree of
independence on both sides.

SAGITTARIUS
AND GEMINI

Given that Gemini's airiness can make
Sagittarius' fire highly combustible,
and Jupiter can find Mercury's
intellectual dexterity occasionally
irritating, it's as well that these are
both mutable, adaptable signs that can
work out their differences.

SAGITTARIUS
AND CANCER

The Moon can help enhance Jupiter's feeling side, and Cancer's nurturing style can be exactly what Sagittarius needs to blossom, just as long as the crab isn't too possessive and clingy, which is often the real challenge to this relationship.

SAGITTARIUS
AND LEO

Although both fire signs, Leo often has an ego that is often too demanding for independently minded Sagittarius to tolerate, and it takes quite a compromise for the Sun to concede to Jupiter too, although they do understand each other.

SAGITTARIUS
AND VIRGO

Both adaptable signs, Virgo has the versatility to adjust to Sagittarius' need for independence and a practical ability to manage their demands for freedom, while balancing their own life, making this a good possibility for Mercury/Jupiter success.

SAGITTARIUS AND LIBRA

Venus and Jupiter often make happy bedfellows, and Libra's instinct for partnership can help balance Sagittarius' need for travel and adventure, and as long as they both have the space they feel they need, this relationship can thrive.

SAGITTARIUS AND SCORPIO

Pluto exerts a regenerative effect that can help reinvent this relationship again and again, ensuring that Sagittarius is seldom bored or loses interest, although the deeper, more spiritual side of Scorpio may always remain a bit of a mystery.

SAGITTARIUS AND SAGITTARIUS

They understand each other and are enthusiastic about all the possibilities of a great life together, but it may come down to whether or not their different needs for exploration and adventure coincide rather than clash.

SAGITTARIUS
AND CAPRICORN

Saturn has the discipline that an errant Jupiter sometimes needs to flourish, but it often requires careful handling by grounded Capricorn to allow Sagittarius the space they need while ensuring their needs too are met for this to work.

SAGITTARIUS
AND AQUARIUS

Airy, humanitarian Aquarius may be the one sign who truly understands Sagittarius' need for emotional freedom, so much so that they can sometimes rather be unpredictable, which certainly keeps this partnership on its toes.

SAGITTARIUS
AND PISCES

Pisces' imagination and creativity intrigues Sagittarius and they have a similar approach to life's plans and ideas. Neptune can be a very harmonious pairing with Jupiter, as long as this gentle water sign calms, but doesn't douse, the fire sign.

SAGITTARIUS
AT WORK

Work is an interesting concept for Sagittarius. Because they are usually so curious and full of ideas, but also independent, it's sometimes hard to see how they can stay still long enough to deliver on anything. Fortunately, ruling the house of travel and the sending out of ideas can include forms of communication, so in these areas – publishing and other forms of media – Sagittarius often excels. As long as their interest is held, Sagittarius will graft, and it's a wise boss who learns to trust this and give their employee the independence to deliver. Plus, Sagittarius is often so charming, they are an asset either to a team or when working alone.

The only caveat is that one job for life is unlikely to satisfy Sagittarius. True, some will explore, develop and expand on a role, going from strength to strength, but for others there may be a variety of career changes over their working life. Money isn't much of a motivator either for most Sagittarius, it's more a question of keeping their enthusiasm fired up. Often they make the best entrepreneurs, as long as they can stick to the boring bits, unless they can partner with someone who is more capable of delivering on the nuts and bolts of the mundane.

Another trait often common to Sagittarius is problem-solving, because they are so often capable of thinking 'outside the box', coming at things from a novel perspective, and this ability can be applied to anything from advertising to science. It just takes a certain amount of application to consider the wider possibilities of work, which Sagittarius often needs to do before they finally find a satisfying workplace.

An obvious career choice for Sagittarius would be within the travel industry. Exploring new and interesting travel destinations, particularly for adventure holidays, would be ideal. Or working within travel journalism. Writing is another way to creatively explore and develop ideas, and this is often a feature of many Sagittarius' careers in one form or another. One thing common to many Sagittarius is their ability to find a good work/life balance. Work is important, yes, and a means to financing life, but Sagittarius naturally veers towards what pleases their soul as much as their bank manager. They know in their heart there's more to life than just work.

SAGITTARIUS
AT HOME

I t's tempting to think that Sagittarius' home is where they lay their hat. True, they can be restless but they also know the value of a home from which they can leave, and return; they also know that if they want to create a home and family, and many do, the bricks and mortar of a home are an important part of this. In addition, although they are not particularly motivated by money, Sagittarius is smart enough to know that if they invest in nothing else, a home isn't a bad option.

Sagittarius are also socially minded and enjoy the company of others. Ruled by Jupiter, Sagittarius likes to extend their hospitality to others, which sometimes needs to be cleared by other housemates, friends or family before someone they've only just met is invited to stay for a month. Their home often showcases items from their travels, each one telling a story of a place visited or people met. Sagittarius' hosting skills might be a little haphazard, and although gourmet dining might be a bit of a stretch, they can rustle up an omelette as well as anyone, and are often happy to share their last crust with a stranger.

One of the least possessive of the sun signs, Sagittarius isn't particularly materialistic or sentimental about possessions. Sagittarius may have no problem with sharing and can be surprised when others do, so there may be some ground to be negotiated between housemates here. In turn, they do like to have their independence respected, so there's room for give and take on both sides. Otherwise, Sagittarius is generally an easy-going, warm-hearted housemate, even if they have a tendency to disappear for a while, forgetting to say they're away for a week's holiday or off for six months travelling.

FREE THE
SPIRIT

Understanding your own sun sign astrology is only part of the picture. It provides you with a template to examine and reflect on your own life's journey but also the context for this through your relationships with others, intimate or otherwise, and within the culture and environment in which you live.

Throughout time, the Sun and planets of our universe have kept to their paths and astrologers have used this ancient wisdom to understand the pattern of the universe. In this way, astrology is a tool to utilise these wisdoms, a way of helping make sense of the energies we experience as the planets shift in our skies.

'A physician without a knowledge of astrology has no right to call himself a physician,' said Hippocrates, the Greek physician born in 460 BC, who understood better than anyone how these psychic energies worked. As did Carl Jung, the 20th-century philosopher and psychoanalyst, because he said, 'Astrology represents the summation of all the psychological knowledge of antiquity.'

SUN

RULES THE ASTROLOGICAL SIGN OF LEO

Although the Sun is officially a star, for the purpose of astrology it's considered a planet. It is also the centre of our universe and gives us both light and energy; our lives are dependent on it and it embodies our creative life force. As a life giver, the Sun is considered a masculine entity, the patriarch and ruler of the skies. Our sun sign is where we start our astrological journey whichever sign it falls in, and as long as we know which day of which month we were born, we have this primary knowledge.

MOON

We now know that the Moon is actually a natural satellite of the Earth (the third planet from the Sun) rather than a planet but is considered such for the purposes of astrology. It's dependent on the Sun for its reflected light, and it is only through their celestial relationship that we can see it. In this way, the Moon in each of our birth charts depicts the feminine energy to balance the masculine Sun's life force, the ying to its yang. It is not an impotent or subservient presence, particularly when you consider how it gives the world's oceans their tides, the relentless energy of the ebb and flow powering up the seas. The Moon's energy also helps illuminate our unconscious desires, helping to bring these to the service of our self-knowledge.

MERCURY

RULES THE ASTROLOGICAL SIGNS OF GEMINI AND VIRGO

Mercury, messenger of the gods, has always been
associated with speed and agility, whether in body
or mind. Because of this, Mercury is considered to
be the planet of quick wit and anything requiring
verbal dexterity and the application of intelligence.
Those with Mercury prominent in their chart love
exchanging and debating ideas and telling stories
(often with a tendency to embellish the truth of a
situation), making them prominent in professions
where these qualities are valuable.

Astronomically, Mercury is the closest planet to the
Sun and moves around a lot in our skies. What's also
relevant is that several times a year Mercury appears
to be retrograde (see page 99) which has the effect of
slowing down or disrupting its influence.

VENUS

RULES THE ASTROLOGICAL SIGNS OF TAURUS AND LIBRA

The goddess of beauty, love and pleasure. Venus is
the second planet from the Sun and benefits from
this proximity, having received its positive vibes.
Depending on which astrological sign Venus falls in
your chart will influence how you relate to art and
culture and the opposite sex. The characteristics of
this sign will tell you all you need to know about
what you aspire to, where you seek and how you
experience pleasure, along with the types of lover you
attract. Again, partly depending on where it's placed,
Venus can sometimes increase self-indulgence which
can be a less positive aspect of a hedonistic life.

MARS

This big, powerful planet is fourth from the Sun
and exerts an energetic force, powering up the
characteristics of the astrological sign in which it
falls in your chart. This will tell you how you assert
yourself, whether your anger flares or smoulders,
what might stir your passion and how you express
your sexual desires. Mars will show you what works
best for you to turn ideas into action, the sort of
energy you might need to see something through
and how your independent spirit can be most
effectively engaged.

JUPITER

RULES THE ASTROLOGICAL SIGN OF SAGITTARIUS

Big, bountiful Jupiter is the largest planet in our solar
system and fifth from the Sun. It heralds optimism,
generosity and general benevolence. Whichever sign
Jupiter falls in in your chart is where you will find
the characteristics for your particular experience of
luck, happiness and good fortune. Jupiter will show
you which areas to focus on to gain the most and
best from your life. Wherever Jupiter appears in your
chart it will bring a positive influence and when it's
prominent in our skies we all benefit.

SATURN

RULES THE ASTROLOGICAL SIGN OF CAPRICORN

Saturn is considered akin to Old Father Time, with all the patience, realism and wisdom that archetype evokes. Sometimes called the taskmaster of the skies, its influence is all about how we handle responsibility and it requires that we graft and apply ourselves in order to learn life's lessons. The sixth planet from the Sun, Saturn's 'return' (see page 100) to its place in an individual's birth chart occurs approximately every 28 years. How self-disciplined you are about overcoming opposition or adversity will be influenced by the characteristics of the sign in which this powerful planet falls in your chart.

URANUS

RULES THE ASTROLOGICAL SIGN OF AQUARIUS

The seventh planet from the Sun, Uranus is the
planet of unpredictability, change and surprise, and
whether you love or loathe the impact of Uranus
will depend in part on which astrological sign it
influences in your chart. How you respond to its
influence is entirely up to the characteristics of the
sign it occupies in your chart. Whether you see the
change it heralds as a gift or a curse is up to you, but
because it takes seven years to travel through a sign,
its presence in a sign can influence a generation.

NEPTUNE

Neptune ruled the sea, and this planet is all about deep waters of mystery, imagination and secrets. It's also representative of our spiritual side so the characteristics of whichever astrological sign it occupies in your chart will influence how this plays out in your life. Neptune is the eighth planet from the Sun and its influence can be subtle and mysterious. The astrological sign in which it falls in your chart will indicate how you realise your vision, dream and goals. The only precaution is if it falls in an equally watery sign, creating a potential difficulty in distinguishing between fantasy and reality.

PLUTO

Pluto is the furthest planet from the Sun and exerts a regenerative energy that transforms but often requires destruction to erase what's come before in order to begin again. Its energy often lies dormant and then erupts, so the astrological sign in which it falls will have a bearing on how this might play out in your chart. Transformation can be very positive but also very painful. When Pluto's influence is strong, change occurs and how you react or respond to this will be very individual. Don't fear it, but reflect on how to use its energy to your benefit.

YOUR SUN SIGN

Your sun or zodiac sign is the one in which you were born, determined by the date of your birth. Your sun sign is ruled by a specific planet. For example, Sagittarius is ruled by Jupiter but Gemini by Mercury, so we already have the first piece of information and the first piece of our individual jigsaw puzzle.

The next piece of the jigsaw is understanding that the energy of a particular planet in your birth chart (see page 78) plays out via the characteristics of the astrological sign in which it's positioned, and this is hugely valuable in understanding some of the patterns of your life. You may have your Sun in Sagittarius, and a good insight into the characteristics of this sign, but what if you have Neptune in Leo? Or Venus in Aries? Uranus in Virgo? Understanding the impact of these influences can help you reflect on the way you react or respond and the choices you can make, helping to ensure more positive outcomes.

If, for example, with Uranus in Taurus you are resistant to change, remind yourself that change is inevitable and can be positive, allowing you to work with it rather than against its influence. If you have Neptune in Virgo, it will bring a more spiritual element to this practical earth sign, while Mercury in Aquarius will enhance the predictive element of your analysis and judgement. The scope and range and useful aspect of having this knowledge is just the beginning of how you can utilise astrology to live your best life.

PLANETS IN TRANSIT

In addition, the planets do not stay still. They are said to transit (move) through the course of an astrological year. Those closest to us, like Mercury, transit quite regularly (every 88 days), while those further away, like Pluto, take much longer, in this case 248 years to come full circle. So the effects of each planet can vary depending on their position and this is why we hear astrologers talk about someone's Saturn return (see page 100), Mercury retrograde (see page 99) or about Capricorn (or other sun sign) 'weather'. This is indicative of an influence that can be anticipated and worked with and is both universal and personal. The shifting positions of the planets bring an influence to bear on each of us, linked to the position of our own planetary influences and how these have a bearing on each other. If you understand the nature of these planetary influences you can begin to work with, rather than against, them and this information can be very much to your benefit. First, though, you need to take a look at the component parts of astrology, the pieces of your personal jigsaw, then you'll have the information you need to make sense of how your sun sign might be affected during the changing patterns of the planets.

YOUR BIRTH CHART

With the date, time and place of birth, you can easily find out where your (or anyone else's) planets are positioned from an online astrological chart programme (see page 110). This will give you an exact sun sign position, which you probably already know, but it can also be useful if you think you were born 'on the cusp' because it will give you an *exact* indication of what sign you were born in. In addition, this natal chart will tell you your Ascendant sign, which sign your Moon is in, along with the other planets specific to your personal and completely individual chart and the Houses (see page 81) in which the astrological signs are positioned.

A birth chart is divided into 12 sections, representing each of the 12 Houses (see pages 82–85) with your Ascendant or Rising sign always positioned in the 1st House, and the other 11 Houses running counter-clockwise from one to 12.

ASCENDANT OR RISING SIGN

Your Ascendant is a first, important part of the complexity of an individual birth chart. While your sun sign gives you an indication of the personality you will inhabit through the course of your life, it is your Ascendant or Rising sign – which is the sign rising at the break of dawn on the Eastern horizon at the time and on the date of your birth – that often gives a truer indication of how you will project your personality and consequently how the world sees you. So even though you were born a sun sign Sagittarius, whatever sign your Ascendant is in, for example Cancer, will be read through the characteristics of this astrological sign.

Your Ascendant is always in your 1st House, which is the House of the Self (see page 82) and the other houses always follow the same consecutive astrological order. So if, for example, your Ascendant is Leo, then your second house is in Virgo, your third house in Libra, and so on. Each house has its own characteristics but how these will play out in your individual chart will be influenced by the sign positioned in it.

Opposite your Ascendant is your Descendant sign, positioned in the 7th House (see page 84) and this shows what you look for in a partnership, your complementary 'other half' as it were. There's always something intriguing about what the Descendant can help us to understand, and it's worth knowing yours and being on the lookout for it when considering a long-term marital or business partnership.

THE
12
HOUSES

While each of the 12 Houses represent different aspects of our lives, they are also ruled by one of the 12 astrological signs, giving each house its specific characteristics. When we discover, for example, that we have Capricorn in the 12th House, this might suggest a pragmatic or practical approach to spirituality. Or, if you had Gemini in your 6th House, this might suggest a rather airy approach to organisation.

1ST HOUSE

RULED BY ARIES

The first impression you give walking into
a room, how you like to be seen, your sense
of self and the energy with which you
approach life.

2ND HOUSE

RULED BY TAURUS

What you value, including what you own
that provides your material security; your
self-value and work ethic, how you earn
your income.

3RD HOUSE

RULED BY GEMINI

How you communicate through words,
deeds and gestures; also how you learn and
function in a group, including within your
own family.

4TH HOUSE

RULED BY CANCER

This is about your home, your security and how you take care of yourself and your family; and also about those family traditions you hold dear.

5TH HOUSE

RULED BY LEO

Creativity in all its forms, including fun and eroticism, intimate relationships and procreation, self-expression and positive fulfilment.

6TH HOUSE

RULED BY VIRGO

How you organise your daily routine, your health, your business affairs, and how you are of service to others, from those in your family to the workplace.

7 TH HOUSE

RULED BY LIBRA

This is about partnerships and shared
goals, whether marital or in business,
and what we look for in these to
complement ourselves.

8 TH HOUSE

RULED BY SCORPIO

Regeneration, through death and rebirth,
and also our legacy and how this might be
realised through sex, procreation
and progeny.

9 TH HOUSE

RULED BY SAGITTARIUS

Our world view, cultures outside our
own and the bigger picture beyond our
immediate horizon, to which we travel
either in body or mind.

10TH HOUSE

RULED BY CAPRICORN

Our aims and ambitions in life, what we aspire to and what we're prepared to do to achieve it; this is how we approach our working lives.

11TH HOUSE

RULED BY AQUARIUS

The house of humanity and our friendships, our relationships with the wider world, our tribe or group to which we feel an affiliation.

12TH HOUSE

RULED BY PISCES

Our spiritual side resides here. Whether this is religious or not, it embodies our inner life, beliefs and the deeper connections we forge.

THE FOUR
ELEMENTS

The 12 astrological signs are divided into four groups, representing the four elements: fire, water, earth and air. This gives each of the three signs in each group additional characteristics.

FIRE

ARIES ❧ LEO ❧ SAGITTARIUS

Embodying warmth, spontaneity and enthusiasm.

WATER

CANCER ❧ SCORPIO ❧ PISCES

Embodying a more feeling, spiritual and intuitive side.

EARTH

TAURUS ❧ VIRGO ❧ CAPRICORN

Grounded and sure-footed and sometimes rather stubborn.

SAGITTARIUS

AIR

GEMINI ~ LIBRA ~ AQUARIUS

Flourishing in the world of vision, ideas and perception.

FIXED,
CARDINAL OR
MUTABLE?

The 12 signs are further divided into three groups of four, giving additional characteristics of being fixed, cardinal or mutable. These represent the way in which they respond to situations.

FIXED

TAURUS, LEO, SCORPIO AND AQUARIUS ARE FIXED SIGNS

Their energy tends to be steady and they are less reactive, more responsive, although they can have a tendency to be resistant to change and need encouragement.

CARDINAL

ARIES, CANCER, LIBRA AND CAPRICORN ARE CARDINAL SIGNS

Their energy is often instinctive and action-oriented, enabling them to get things started, although there's sometimes a tendency to fail to carry things through.

MUTABLE

GEMINI, VIRGO, SAGITTARIUS AND PISCES ARE MUTABLE SIGNS

The clue here is their adaptability and responsiveness to change, which they don't fear, and readiness to listen to and embrace new ideas.

MERCURY RETROGRADE

This occurs several times over the astrological year and lasts for around four weeks, with a shadow week either side (a quick Google search will tell you the forthcoming dates). It's important what sign Mercury is in while it's retrograde, because its impact will be affected by the characteristics of that sign. For example, if Mercury is retrograde in Gemini, the sign of communication that is ruled by Mercury, the effect will be keenly felt in all areas of communication. However, if Mercury is retrograde in Aquarius, which rules the house of friendships and relationships, this may keenly affect our communication with large groups, or if in Sagittarius, which rules the house of travel, it could affect travel itineraries and encourage us to check our documents carefully.

Mercury retrograde can also be seen as an opportunity to pause, review or reconsider ideas and plans, to regroup, recalibrate and recuperate, and generally to take stock of where we are and how we might proceed. In our fast-paced 24/7 lives, Mercury retrograde can often be a useful opportunity to slow down and allow ourselves space to restore some necessary equilibrium.

SATURN RETURN

When the planet Saturn returns to the place in your chart that it occupied at the time of your birth, it has an impact. This occurs roughly every 28 years, so we can see immediately that it correlates with ages that we consider representative of different life stages and when we might anticipate change or adjustment to a different era. At 28 we can be considered at full adult maturity, probably established in our careers and relationships, maybe with children; at 56 we have reached middle age and are possibly at another of life's crossroads; and at 84, we might be considered at the full height of our wisdom, our lives almost complete. If you know the time and place of your birth date, an online Saturn return calculator can give you the exact timing.

It will also be useful to identify in which astrological sign Saturn falls in your chart, which will help you reflect on its influence, as both influences can be very illuminating about how you will experience and manage the impact of its return. Often the time leading up to a personal Saturn return is a demanding one, but the lessons learnt help inform the decisions made about how to progress your own goals. Don't fear this period, but work with its influence: knowledge is power and Saturn has a powerful energy you can harness should you choose.

  ✈

THE MINOR
PLANETS

Sun sign astrology seldom makes mention of these 'minor' planets that also orbit the Sun, but increasingly their subtle influence is being referenced. If you have had your birth chart done (if you know your birth time and place you can do this online) you will have access to this additional information.

Like the 10 main planets on the previous pages, these 18 minor entities will also be positioned in an astrological sign, bringing their energy to bear on these characteristics. You may, for example, have Fortuna in Leo, or Diana in Sagittarius. Look to these for their subtle influences on your birth chart and life via the sign they inhabit, all of which will serve to animate and resonate further the information you can reference on your own personal journey.

AESCULAPIA

Jupiter's grandson and a powerful
healer, Aesculapia was taught by
Chiron and influences us in what
could be life-saving action, realised
through the characteristics of the sign
in which it falls in our chart.

BACCHUS

Jupiter's son, Bacchus is similarly
benevolent but can sometimes lack
restraint in the pursuit of pleasure.
How this plays out in your chart is
dependent on the sign in which
it falls.

APOLLO

Jupiter's son, gifted in art, music and
healing, Apollo rides the Sun across
the skies. His energy literally lights up
the way in which you inspire others,
characterised by the sign in which it
falls in your chart.

CERES

Goddess of agriculture and mother of
Proserpina, Ceres is associated with
the seasons and how we manage cycles
of change in our lives. This energy is
influenced by the sign in which it falls
in our chart.

CHIRON

Teacher of the gods, Chiron knew all about healing herbs and medical practices and he lends his energy to how we tackle the impossible or the unthinkable, that which seems difficult to do.

DIANA

Jupiter's independent daughter was allowed to run free without the shackles of marriage. Where this falls in your birth chart will indicate what you are not prepared to sacrifice in order to conform.

CUPID

Son of Venus. The sign into which Cupid falls will influence how you inspire love and desire in others, not always appropriately and sometimes illogically but it can still be an enduring passion.

FORTUNA

Jupiter's daughter, who is always shown blindfolded, influences your fated role in other people's lives, how you show up for them without really understanding why, and at the right time.

HYGEIA

Daughter of Aesculapia and also associated with health, Hygeia is about how you anticipate risk and the avoidance of unwanted outcomes. The way you do this is characterised by the sign in which Hygeia falls.

MINERVA

Another of Jupiter's daughters, depicted by an owl, will show you via the energy given to a particular astrological sign in your chart how you show up at your most intelligent and smart. How you operate intellectually.

JUNO

Juno was the wife of Jupiter and her position in your chart will indicate where you will make a commitment in order to feel safe and secure. It's where you might seek protection in order to flourish.

OPS

The wife of Saturn, Ops saved the life of her son Jupiter by giving her husband a stone to eat instead of him. Her energy in our chart enables us to find positive solutions to life's demands and dilemmas.

PANACEA

Gifted with healing powers, Panacea
provides us with a remedy for all ills
and difficulties, and how this plays
out in your life will depend on the
characteristics of the astrological sign
in which her energy falls.

PSYCHE

Psyche, Venus' daughter-in-law, shows
us that part of ourselves that is easy to
love and endures through adversity,
and your soul that survives death and
flies free, like the butterfly that
depicts her.

PROSERPINA

Daughter of Ceres, abducted by Pluto,
Proserpina has to spend her life divided
between earth and the underworld and
she represents how we bridge the gulf
between different and difficult aspects
of our lives.

SALACIA

Neptune's wife, Salacia stands on
the seashore bridging land and sea,
happily bridging the two realities.
In your chart, she shows how you
can harmoniously bring two sides of
yourself together.

VESTA

Daughter of Saturn, Vesta's job was
to protect Rome and in turn she
was protected by vestal virgins. Her
energy influences how we manage our
relationships with competitive females
and male authority figures.

VULCAN

Vulcan was a blacksmith who knew
how to control fire and fashion metal
into shape, and through the sign in
which it falls in your chart will show
you how you control your passion and
make it work for you.

FURTHER READING

Jung's Studies in Astrology: Prophecies, Magic and the Qualities of Time,

Liz Greene, Routledge (2018)

Lunar Oracle: Harness the Power of the Moon,

Liberty Phi, OH Editions (2021)

Metaphysics of Astrology: Why Astrology Works,

Ivan Antic, Independently published (2020)

Parkers' Astrology: The Definitive Guide to Using Astrology in Every Aspect of Your Life,

Julia and Derek Parker, Dorling Kindersley (2020)

USEFUL WEBSITES

Alicebellastrology.com
Astro.com
Astrology.com
Cafeastrology.com
Costarastrology.com
Jessicaadams.com

USEFUL APPS

Astro Future
Co-Star
Moon
Sanctuary
Time Nomad
Time Passages

ACKNOWLEDGEMENTS

Thanks are due to my Taurean publisher Kate Pollard for commissioning this Astrology Oracle series, to Piscean Matt Tomlinson for his careful editing, and to Evi O Studio for their beautiful design and illustrations.

ABOUT THE AUTHOR

As a sun sign Aquarius Liberty Phi loves to explore the world and has lived on three different continents, currently residing in North America. Their Gemini moon inspires them to communicate their love of astrology and other esoteric practices while Leo rising helps energise them. Their first publication, also released by OH Editions, is a box set of 36 oracle cards and accompanying guide, entitled *Lunar Oracle: Harness the Power of the Moon*.

Published in 2023 by OH Editions,
an imprint of Welbeck Non-Fiction Ltd,
part of the Welbeck Publishing Group.
Offices in London, 20 Mortimer Street, London, W1T 3JW,
and Sydney, 205 Commonwealth Street, Surry Hills, 2010.
www.welbeckpublishing.com

Design © 2023 OH Editions
Text © 2023 Liberty Phi
Illustrations © 2023 Evi O. Studio

A CIP catalogue record for this book is available from the British Library.

ISBN 978-1-80453-001-6

Publisher: Kate Pollard
Editor: Sophie Elletson
In-house editor: Matt Tomlinson
Designer: Evi O. Studio
Illustrator: Evi O. Studio
Production controller: Jess Brisley
Printed and bound by Leo Paper